HOW TO DRAW...™

WALES

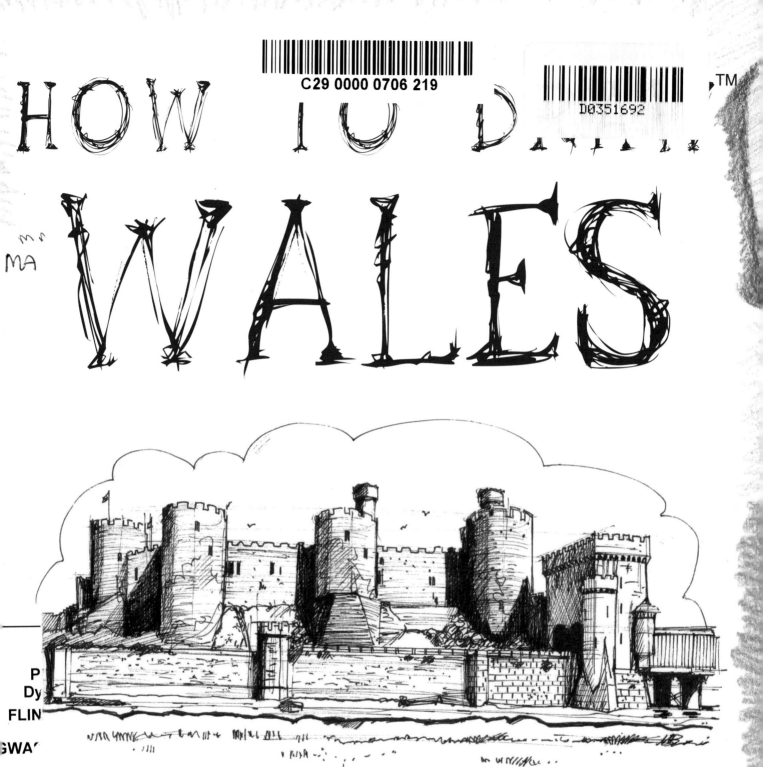

Mark Bergin

BOOK HOUSE

SALARIYA

Published in Great Britain in MMXV by
Book House, an imprint of
The Salariya Book Company Ltd
25 Marlborough Place, Brighton BN1 1UB

1 3 5 7 9 8 6 4 2

Author: **Mark Bergin** was born in Hastings in 1961. He
studied at Eastbourne College of Art and has specialised in
historical reconstructions as well as aviation and maritime
subjects since 1983. He lives in Bexhill-on-Sea with his
wife and three children.

Editors: Rob Walker, Caroline (

PB ISBN: 978-1-909645-56-1

A CIP catalogue record for this
book is available from the
British Library.

Printed and bound in China.
Printed on paper from
sustainable sources.

FLINTSHIRE SIR Y FFLINT	
C29 0000 0706 219	
Askews & Holts	03-Mar-2015
J743.899429	£5.99
MA	

**WARNING: Fixatives should be used
only under adult supervision.**

Visit our websites to read
interactive **free** web books, stay up
to date with new releases, catch
up with us on the
Book House Blog, view our
electronic catalogue and more!

www.salariya.com
Free electronic versions of four of
our *You Wouldn't Want to Be* titles

www.book-house.co.uk
Online catalogue
Information books
and graphic novels

www.scribobooks.com
Fiction books

www.scribblersbooks.com
Books for babies, toddlers and
pre-school children

**www.flickr.com/photos/
salariyabookhouse**
View our photostream with sneak
previews of forthcoming titles

Join the conversation on Facebook
and Twitter by visiting
www.salariya.com

Visit our YouTube channel to see
Mark Bergin doing step-by-step
illustrations:
**www.youtube.com/user/
theSalariya**

Visit
www.salariya.com
for our online catalogue and
free interactive web books.

PAPER FROM
SUSTAINABLE
FORESTS

Contents

Making a start

Learning to draw is about looking and seeing. Keep practising and use a sketchbook to make quick drawings. Start by doodling, and experiment with shapes and patterns. There are many ways to draw, and this book shows only some of them. Visit art galleries, look at artists' drawings and see how friends draw, but above all, find your own way.

Princes of Wales' feathers

Keep a sketchbook handy at all times. Practise recording the main details of an object or scene. This will help you to become more analytical when drawing.

Use basic shapes and construction lines to make quick sketches that capture the essence of a scene.

Pentre Ifan

Practice makes perfect. If your first attempt doesn't look right, don't be afraid to start again.

Welsh Cottage

Look carefully at buildings to study the different textures of stone, bricks and wood.

The Great Orme

Use the white of the paper to create water reflections and breaking waves.

5

Drawing materials

Try using different types of drawing paper and materials. Experiment with charcoal, wax crayons and pastels. All pens, from felt-tips to ballpoints, will make interesting marks — you could also try drawing with pen and ink on wet paper.

Pastels come in a wide range of colours. They are incredibly soft and are easily smudged. Use fixative to protect the drawing.

Silhouette is a style of drawing that shows only a solid black shape, like a shadow.

Lines drawn in **ink** cannot be erased, so keep your ink drawings sketchy and less rigid. Don't worry about mistakes, as these lines can be lost in the drawing as it develops.

Soft pencils are graded from B, 2B, 3B, 4B and 5B up to 6B (the softest). HB is between H and B.

Hard pencils are greyer and soft pencils are blacker. Hard pencils are usually graded from 6H (the hardest) through 5H, 4H, 3H and 2H to H.

7

Perspective

If you look at any object from different viewpoints, you will see that the parts that are closest to you look larger, and the parts that are further away look smaller. Perspective drawing uses this effect to create a feeling of depth. It is a way of suggesting three dimensions on a flat drawing surface.

Placing the viewpoint at ground level creates the impression of looking up at the tram.

The vanishing point (V.P.) is the place in a perspective drawing where parallel lines appear to meet. Simple one-point perspective uses only one V.P.

V.P.

8

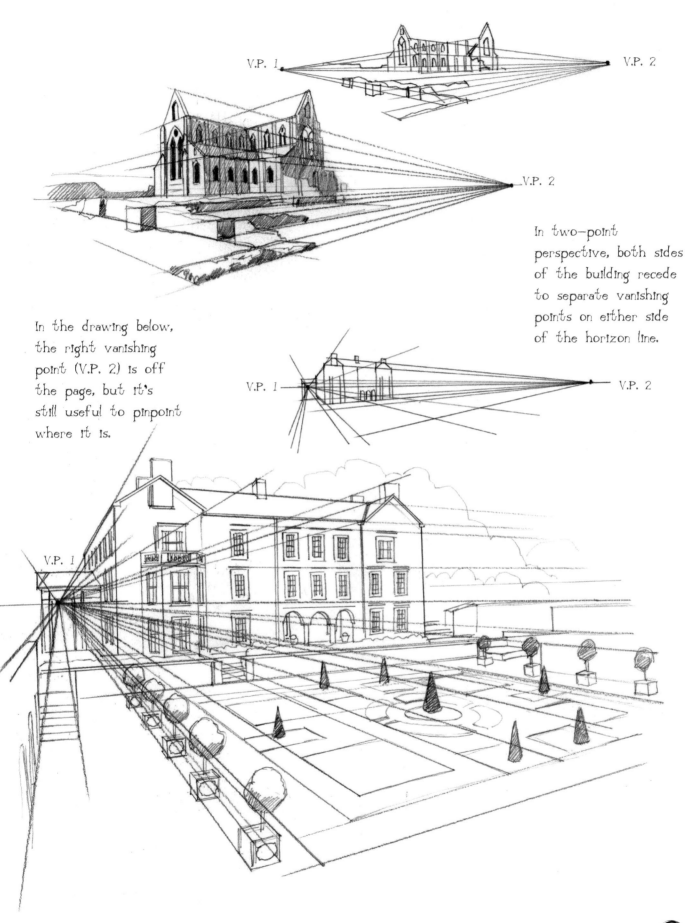

V.P. 1

V.P. 2

V.P. 2

In two-point perspective, both sides of the building recede to separate vanishing points on either side of the horizon line.

In the drawing below, the right vanishing point (V.P. 2) is off the page, but it's still useful to pinpoint where it is.

V.P. 1

V.P. 2

V.P. 1

9

Using photos

Drawing from photographs is a good way to practise drawing a location and it's useful if you don't have time, or it's raining! Drawing from photographs can also help improve your eye for detail.

Choose a good photograph and trace it. Now draw a grid of squares over it.

Now take a piece of drawing paper of the same proportions and draw another grid with the same amount of squares. At this stage, you can enlarge or reduce your drawing by changing the size of the squares. Now carefully copy the shapes in each square of the tracing onto the drawing paper.

Once the outline of the shape is complete, add more details to the drawing. Keep referring to your tracing grid for accuracy.

Light source

To make your drawing look three-dimensional, decide which side the light is coming from, then add shade and tone to the drawing. Areas where light does not reach should be shaded darker.

11

The Welsh flag

The Welsh flag famously pictures the red dragon along with the Tudor colours of green and white. The design of the flag we see today was first shown at the Battle of Bosworth Field in 1485 by the Tudor king, Henry VII.

Start by drawing two ovals for the body (one slightly larger). Connect them with curved lines.

Draw a small circle for the head and add curved lines for the neck.

Sketch in the muzzle.

Draw in the dragon's legs using simple shapes.

Add ovals for the feet.

Add a curled tail with an arrow-shaped end.

Draw in ovals for the toes and add claws. Add an extra claw shape to the back of each leg.

Add the arrow-shaped tongue.

Draw in two pointed ears and horn shapes to the muzzle and to the back of the head.

Draw in the dragon's wing using curved lines. The wing is webbed, like a bat wing.

Add shading to the dragon.

Complete the flag by adding a rectangular border with a central horizontal line running behind the dragon.

Remove any unwanted construction lines.

Welsh National Dress

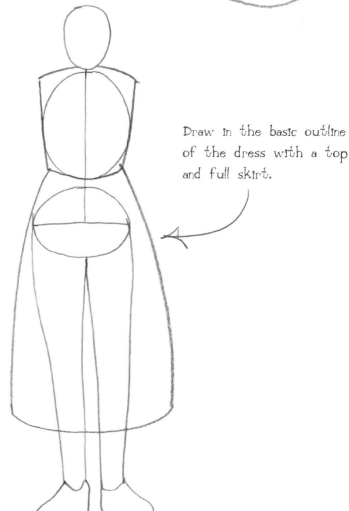

The National Dress of Wales is worn on celebratory occasions. The red cloak and tall black hat are both elements of the costume traditionally worn by rural women of Wales in the 18th century.

Draw three ovals for the head, upper body and hips. Add a line through the centre and a horizontal line across bottom oval for the hips.

Draw in two legs and basic shapes for the feet.

Draw in the basic outline of the dress with a top and full skirt.

Use simple curved lines to add detail to the clothing.

Draw in the arms, hands and a basket.

Sketch in the facial details and add a tall hat.

Draw in the shawl and all remaining details to the costume, including the shoes.

Add shading but leave the apron white.

Add shadows under the skirt and basket (as shown).

Remove any unwanted construction lines.

15

Green Bridge of Wales

The Green Bridge of Wales is a famous Welsh landmark. It is a limestone arch located on the coast of Pembrokeshire. The arch has formed by thousands of years of erosion by the sea. It will eventually collapse.

Horizon line.

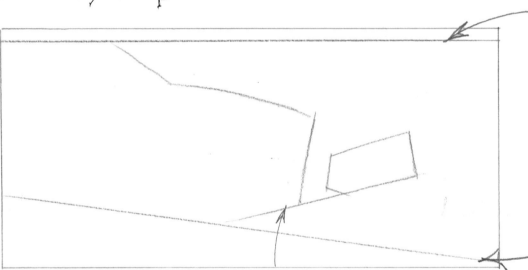

Draw a rectangular box and add the horizon line and a diagonal line for the foreground.

Add basic shapes for the cliffs and rocks beyond.

Sketch in jagged edges for the cliffs that recede to the horizon line.

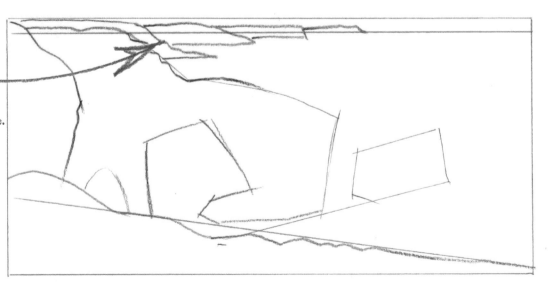

Start adding tone to darker areas where light does not reach.

Light source.

Light source.

Add more detail, including short lines in the foreground to indicate the grassy verge.

Add shadows cast by the rocks.

Shade in the sea, leaving white areas to show the waves breaking around the base of the rocks.

Finish off all details, keeping some areas white to create greater contrast.

Remove any unwanted construction lines.

17

Welsh Rugby players

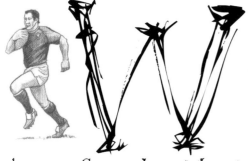

Wales is famous for its love of rugby. The Wales national rugby team has won the Six Nations Championship 26 times and also takes part in the Rugby World Cup.

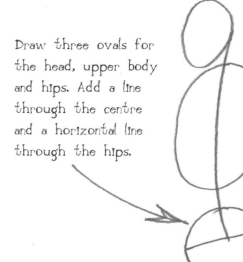

Draw three ovals for the head, upper body and hips. Add a line through the centre and a horizontal line through the hips.

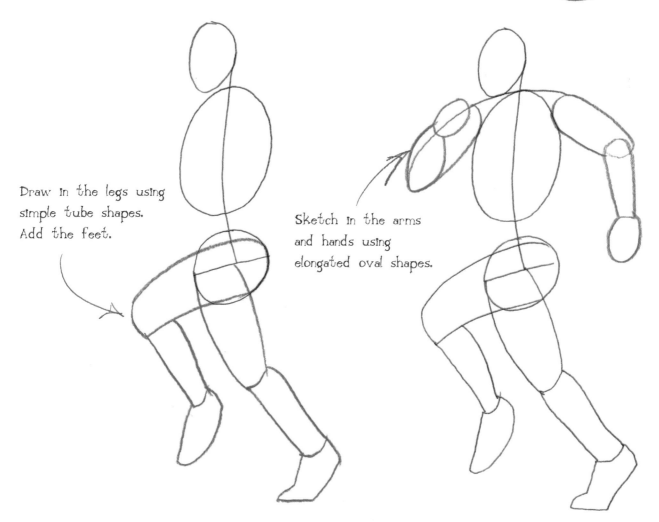

Draw in the legs using simple tube shapes. Add the feet.

Sketch in the arms and hands using elongated oval shapes.

Add details to the face.

Draw in the shirt and add a rugby ball tucked into the body.

Draw in the fingers.

Draw in the facial features and the hairline. Add fingers clutching the ball.

Draw three diagonal lines across the body to create the folds in the shirt. These will need darker shading.

Draw in the shorts, socks and boots.

Decide on the direction of your light source and add shade to areas where light wouldn't reach. Finish off all details.

Remove any unwanted construction lines.

19

Cardiff Castle

Cardiff Castle is renowned for its rich and varied history. It was built in the 11th century on the site of a Roman fort, and its tunnels served as air raid shelters during World War II. Located in Cardiff, the capital of Wales, it is one of the country's most visited castles.

Start by drawing in the castle mound (as shown).

Add diagonal lines for the stairs.

Draw in the basic shape of the castle with a series of rectangles.

Draw a horizontal line around the central tower for the battlements and add a turret.

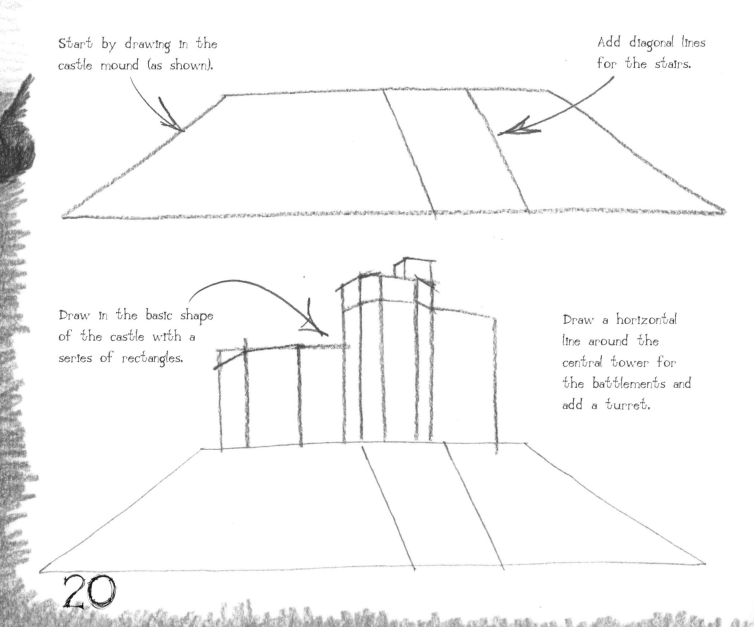

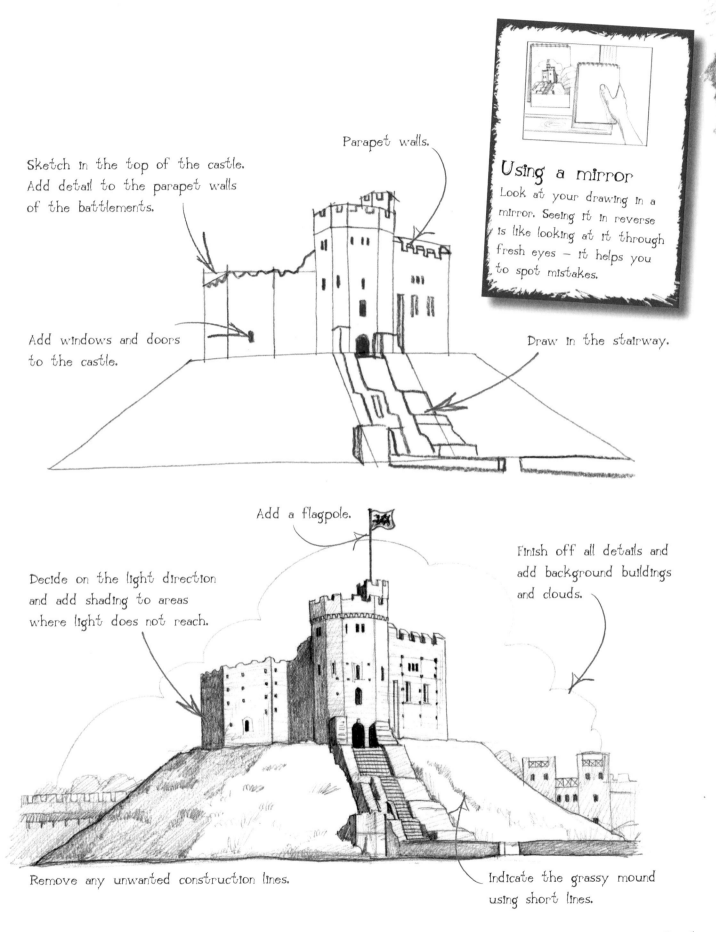

Sketch in the top of the castle. Add detail to the parapet walls of the battlements.

Parapet walls.

Using a mirror
Look at your drawing in a mirror. Seeing it in reverse is like looking at it through fresh eyes — it helps you to spot mistakes.

Add windows and doors to the castle.

Draw in the stairway.

Add a flagpole.

Finish off all details and add background buildings and clouds.

Decide on the light direction and add shading to areas where light does not reach.

Remove any unwanted construction lines.

Indicate the grassy mound using short lines.

21

Caernarfon Castle

Caernarfon Castle is located in North Wales. It dates back to 1283 when King Edward I chose to build his castle here on the site of a former motte and bailey castle. This vast stone structure helped maintain and strengthen the king's power over Wales.

Start by drawing horizontal lines for the base of the castle.

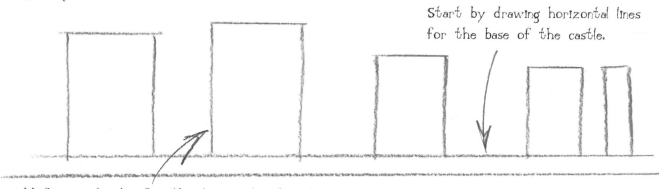

Add five rectangles for the towers (as shown).

Draw in lines to create the three-dimensional structure of the towers.

Draw in the walls that connect all five towers.

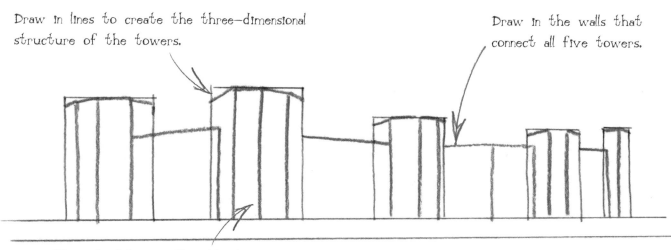

Add vertical lines within the towers.

Draw in horizontal lines to divide the structure (as shown). Add some turrets above.

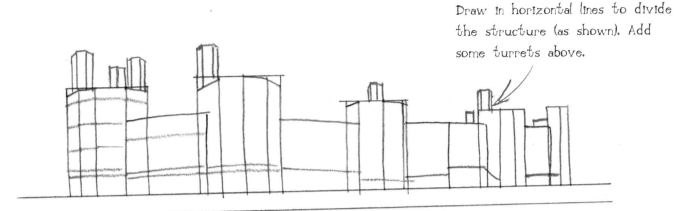

Add flagpoles to the turrets. Draw in squared—off battlements at the top of the castle walls.

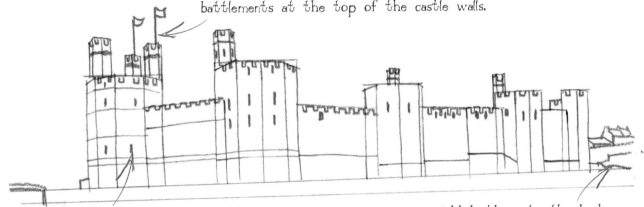

Draw in the windows and add detail to the turrets.

Add buildings to the background.

Draw boats in the foreground for added interest.

Decide on the light direction and add shading to areas light does not reach.

Finish off by adding clouds to the background.

Remove any unwanted construction lines.

23

Mount Snowdon

Mount Snowdon is located in Snowdonia National Park in Gwynedd. At 1085 metres, it is the highest mountain in Wales. Many rare plants flourish in its unique environment formed millions of years ago, out of volcanic rock. The mountain attracts many tourists and rock climbers.

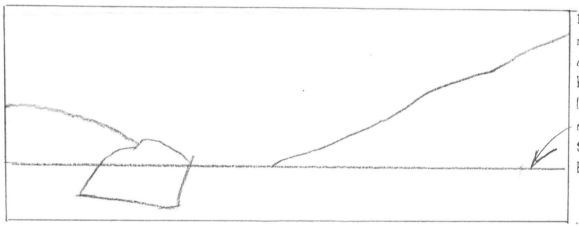

Draw a rectangle and add a horizontal base line for the mountain range. Sketch in basic shapes.

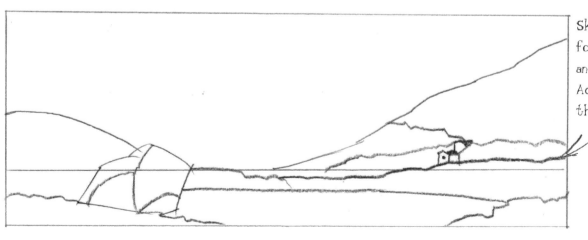

Sketch in the foreground, lake and shoreline. Add detail to the scene.

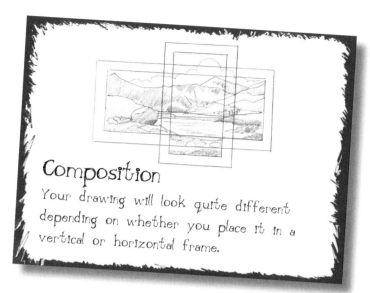

Composition

Your drawing will look quite different depending on whether you place it in a vertical or horizontal frame.

Add the mountain range in the background.
Sketch in the structure of the rock face.

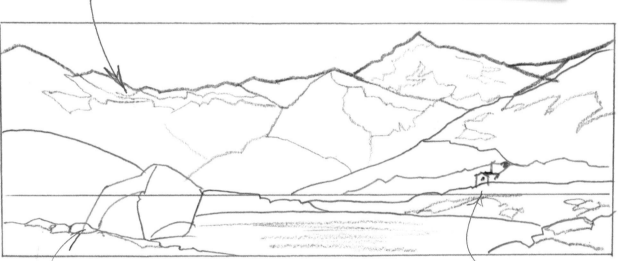

Sketch in some smaller rocks in the foreground.

Add small dwellings.

The light source is coming from the left. Shade in the mountains and rocks where light does not reach.

Leave areas of white paper to create dramatic contrast.

Remove any unwanted construction lines.

25

Tenby Harbour

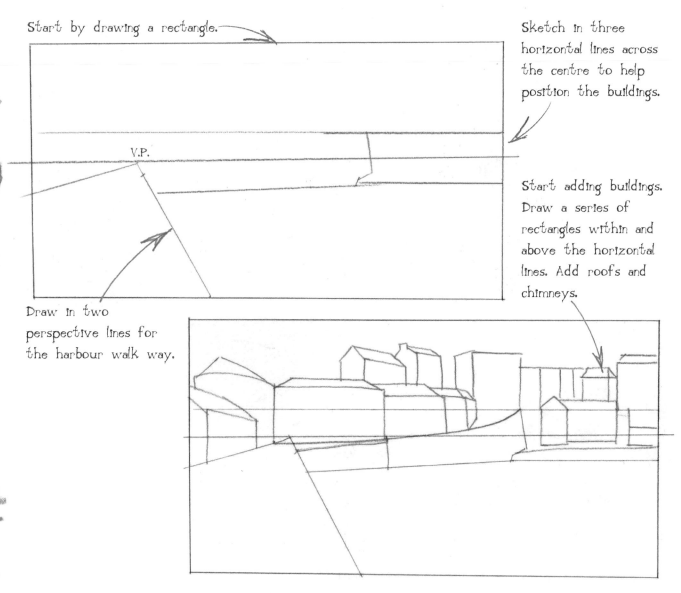

Tenby harbour is a very popular holiday destination in Wales. Tenby, set on top of a hill in Pembrokeshire, has beautiful views of Caldey Island. The ruins of the old town walls date back to medieval times when Tenby was a settlement with a castle.

Start by drawing a rectangle.

Sketch in three horizontal lines across the centre to help position the buildings.

V.P.

Start adding buildings. Draw a series of rectangles within and above the horizontal lines. Add roofs and chimneys.

Draw in two perspective lines for the harbour walk way.

Draw in windows and doors and add more chimneys.

Add more details: lamp posts and bollards to the pathway, trees in the background and stairs leading down to the sea.

Draw boats of various sizes in the harbour.

Add shading to areas where light does not reach. Darken the windows and doors.

Add tone to the sea. Leave some areas white to create reflections in the water.

Add all remaining details to complete.

Remove any unwanted construction lines.

Millennium Centre

The Millennium Centre in Cardiff is one of the most famous landmarks in Wales. Since its opening in 2004, the arts centre has staged numerous opera, ballet, dance and musical performances.

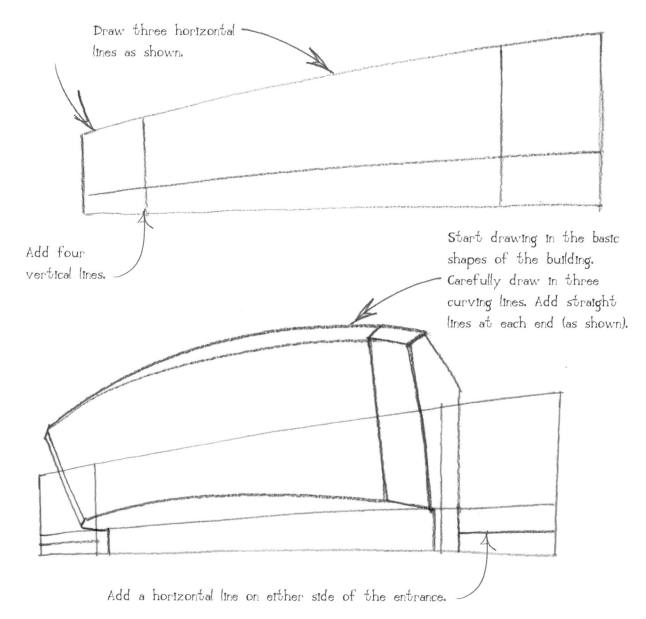

Draw three horizontal lines as shown.

Add four vertical lines.

Start drawing in the basic shapes of the building. Carefully draw in three curving lines. Add straight lines at each end (as shown).

Add a horizontal line on either side of the entrance.

Draw in six more curved lines and add lettering.

Draw horizontal lines on both sides of the building.

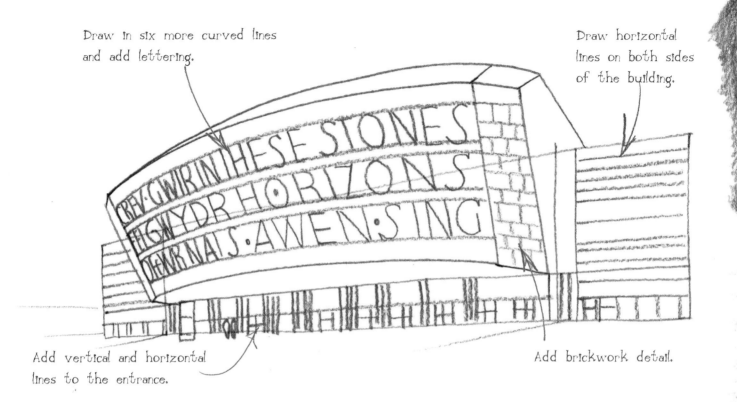

Add vertical and horizontal lines to the entrance.

Add brickwork detail.

Add clouds and buildings to the background for added interest.

Add shading to the building. The underside of the frontage and the lettering will be much darker.

Complete all detail to finish.

Remove any unwanted construction lines.

29

National Botanic Garden

The National Botanic Garden in Wales is famous for its single–spanned glasshouse, the largest structure of its kind in the world. The garden, a centre for botanical research and conservation attracts many visitors.

Start by drawing the asymmetrical domed shape using curved lines. The left side extends to a point.

Add another curved line behind.

Sketch in two more curved lines within the dome.

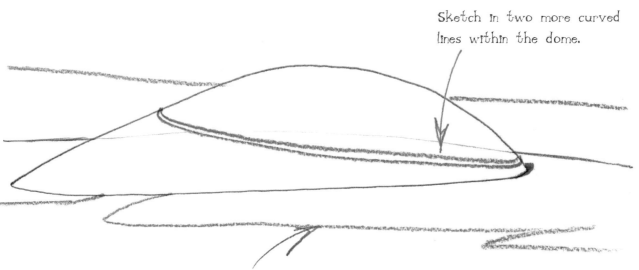

Start indicating the foreground and background areas.

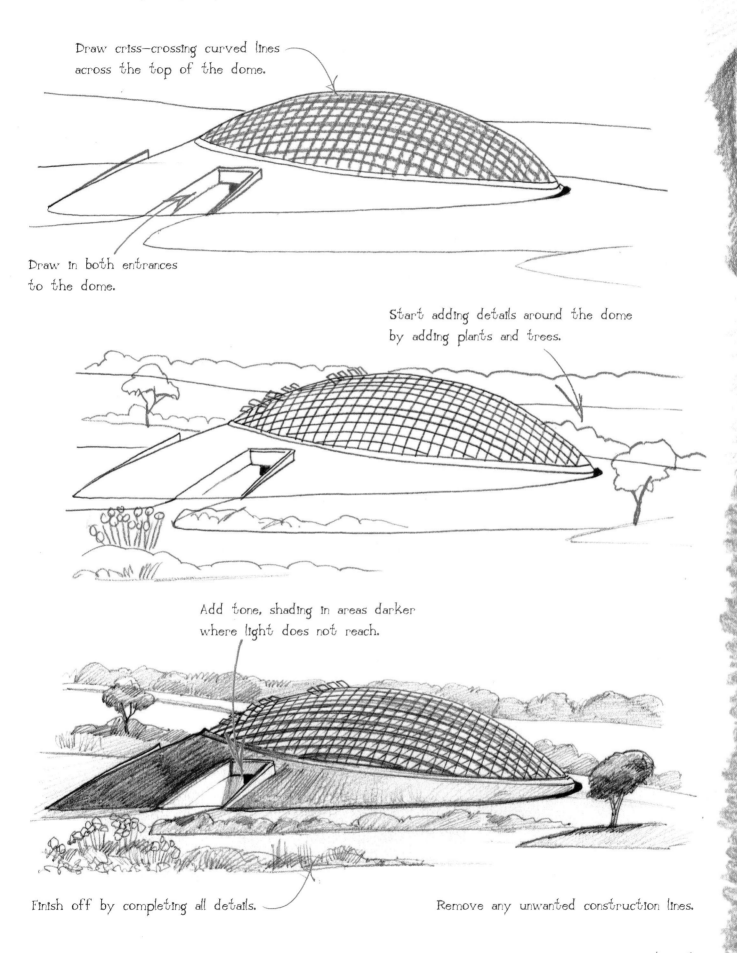

Draw criss-crossing curved lines across the top of the dome.

Draw in both entrances to the dome.

Start adding details around the dome by adding plants and trees.

Add tone, shading in areas darker where light does not reach.

Finish off by completing all details.

Remove any unwanted construction lines.

31

Glossary

Composition The arrangement of the parts of a picture on the drawing paper.

Construction lines Guidelines used in the early stages of a drawing; they may be erased later.

Fixative A type of resin sprayed over a drawing to prevent smudging. **It should only be used by an adult.**

Light source The direction from which the light seems to come in a drawing.

Perspective A method of drawing in which near objects are shown larger than faraway objects to give an impression of depth.

Proportion The correct relationship of scale between each part of the drawing.

Silhouette A drawing that shows only a flat dark shape, like a shadow.

Vanishing point (V.P.) The place in a perspective drawing where parallel lines appear to meet.

Index